A Note from
Mary Pope Osborne About the

When I write Magic Tree House® adventures, I love including facts about the times and places Jack and Annie visit. But when readers finish these adventures, I want them to learn even more. So that's why my husband, Will, and my sister, Natalie Pope Boyce, and I write a series of nonfiction books that are companions to the fiction titles in the Magic Tree House® series. We call these books Fact Trackers because we love to track the facts! Whether we're researching dinosaurs, pyramids, Pilgrims, sea monsters, or cobras, we're always amazed at how wondrous and surprising the real world is. We want you to experience the same wonder we do—so get out your pencils and notebooks and hit the trail with us. You can be a Magic Tree House® Fact Tracker, too!

Mary Pope Osborne

Here's what kids, parents, and teachers have to say about the Magic Tree House® Fact Trackers:

"They are so good. I can't wait for the next one. All I can say for now is prepare to be amazed!" —Alexander N.

"I have read every Magic Tree House book there is. The [Fact Trackers] are a thrilling way to get more information about the special events in the story." —John R.

"These are fascinating nonfiction books that enhance the magical time-traveling adventures of Jack and Annie. I love these books, especially *American Revolution*. I was learning so much, and I didn't even know it!" —Tori Beth S.

"[They] are an excellent 'behind-the-scenes' look at what the [Magic Tree House fiction] has started in your imagination! You can't buy one without the other; they are such a complement to one another." —Erika N., mom

"Magic Tree House [Fact Trackers] took my children on a journey from Frog Creek, Pennsylvania, to so many significant historical events! The detailed manuals are a remarkable addition to the classic fiction Magic Tree House books we adore!" —Jenny S., mom

"[They] are very useful tools in my classroom, as they allow for students to be part of the planning process. Together, we find facts in the [Fact Trackers] to extend the learning introduced in the fictional companions. Researching and planning classroom activities, such as our class Olympics based on facts found in *Ancient Greece and the Olympics*, help create a genuine love for learning!" —Paula H., teacher

Magic Tree House®
Fact Tracker

CHINA: LAND OF THE EMPEROR'S GREAT WALL

A nonfiction companion to
Magic Tree House® #14:
Day of the Dragon King

by Mary Pope Osborne
and Natalie Pope Boyce

illustrated by Carlo Molinari

A STEPPING STONE BOOK™
Random House 🏠 New York

Text copyright © 2014 by Mary Pope Osborne and Natalie Pope Boyce
Interior illustrations copyright © 2014 by Random House LLC
Cover photograph copyright © by Best View Stock/Getty Images

The Magic Tree House Fact Tracker series was formerly known as the Magic
Tree House Research Guide series.

Visit us on the Web!
SteppingStonesBooks.com
MagicTreeHouse.com

Educators and librarians, for a variety of teaching tools, visit us at
RHTeachersLibrarians.com

Library of Congress Cataloging-in-Publication Data
Osborne, Mary Pope.
China : land of the emperor's Great Wall / by Mary Pope Osborne and Natalie
Pope Boyce ; illustrated by Carlo Molinari.
p. cm. — (Magic tree house fact tracker) (A stepping stone book)
"A nonfiction companion to Magic Tree House #14: *Day of the Dragon King*."
ISBN 978-0-385-38635-7 (trade) — ISBN 978-0-385-38636-4 (lib. bdg.) —
ISBN 978-0-385-38637-1 (ebook)
1. China—Juvenile literature. I. Boyce, Natalie Pope. II. Molinari, Carlo,
illustrator. III. Title.
DS706.O79 2015 951—dc23 2014014440

Printed in the United States of America
10 9 8 7 6 5 4 3 2 1

This book has been officially leveled by using the F&P Text Level Gradient™
Leveling System.

To Jennifer Haas,
with love

Historical Consultant:

KENNETH HAMMOND, Professor of History and Director of the
Confucius Institute, New Mexico State University

Education Consultant:

HEIDI JOHNSON, language acquisition and science education specialist,
Bisbee, Arizona

Special thanks to Mallory Loehr, Paula Sadler, Jenna Lettice, Heather Palisi,
Carlo Molinari, and most especially to our patient and excellent editor,
Diane Landolf

CHINA

Contents

Dear Readers,

In <u>Day of the Dragon King</u>, we learned that China has a long history of powerful emperors, amazing inventions, and beautiful art. We wanted to know a lot more about this interesting country.

We discovered that Qin Shihuangdi, the first emperor of all China, began building the Great Wall over 2,000 years ago. The emperor was a strong but harsh ruler. He made thousands of his subjects work on the wall. So many of them died that people called it the cemetery wall. We also learned about the changes he made to unite his country. But best of all, we found out about the emperor's amazing tomb and its terra-cotta army!

We researched a lot more about China and learned it was the first country to invent many things, like the compass, gunpowder, the printing press, and the kite!

Then we studied why Chinese people keep many of their old customs and how hard they work to build a strong country.

So get out your chopsticks and pack some good walking shoes. Let's sail to China and explore the Great Wall together!

Jack
Annie

1

Land of the Emperor's Great Wall

China is a huge country on the continent of Asia. More people live there than in any other nation. In fact, one out of every five people on the planet lives in China.

China's eastern and southeastern coasts are along the Yellow Sea and the China Sea, which are part of the Pacific Ocean.

Mountains take up a third of the country. To the south and southwest are the great

Himalayan mountains, which separate China from India, Nepal, and Bhutan.

Besides its snow-covered mountains, China has high plateaus and great rivers.

The tallest mountains in the world are in the Himalayas.

The mighty Yangtze and Yellow Rivers flow down from the west into the ocean.

The Yangtze stretches almost 4,000 miles. It's the third-longest river in the world. Boats loaded with coal and other

China is about the size of the United States.

goods travel the Yangtze all the way to the East China Sea.

The Gobi and the Taklamakan (tah-kluh-muh-KAHN) Deserts cover a huge part of China's north and west. The Gobi is the biggest desert in Asia. Temperatures there can shoot up to 104 degrees

People often ride camels across the desert.

Fahrenheit during the day and plunge to 40 degrees at night.

The Taklamakan is a very dry desert with venomous snakes, super-hot days, and freezing nights. The Taklamakan is so scary that people call it the Sea of Death.

The Countryside

Half of all Chinese live in the country-side. Many of them work on farms. Not much land is good for farming, but China grows more rice than any other country. Rice has been a basic part of the diet there for about 9,000 years. It is grown in wet fields called rice paddies.

Because there is so little farmland, for centuries people have grown crops

The richest soil in China is near the rivers.

 Terraces are like giant steps.
People plant crops on the flat parts.

on terraces that they have cut from the hillsides.

18

The Chinese often cope with droughts (DROWTZ) that last for several years. At times, people can't get enough food to eat or water to drink. Millions have died during bad droughts.

A drought is when it doesn't rain for a long time and the earth gets very dry.

Since the best land is usually near rivers, floods are also a concern. Life can be hard in the countryside. Every year, many people leave to look for work in the cities.

The Cities

Busy cities like Hong Kong, Beijing, and Shanghai are packed with cars, trucks, motorcycles, and bicycles. Millions of people jam the sidewalks and subways. Since there aren't enough places to live, people often cram into small apartments.

Shanghai is the largest city in China.

The country is one of the top producers of goods sold around the world.

Factories seem to be everywhere. They turn out clothing, electronics, iron, steel, cars, and more. Factories, coal-burning electric plants, and a large number of cars pollute the air. So China has some of the worst pollution in the world.

An Ancient Past

China has a very long history. Some of the earliest settlers probably went to the northeastern part of the country in about 50,000 BC. They were a Stone Age people who lived in caves, wore animal skins, and hunted animals for food.

Owl-shaped Stone Age bowl

Around 4,000 BC, people began moving into central China near the rivers so they could grow crops. They settled in small villages and made weapons and other objects out of bronze.

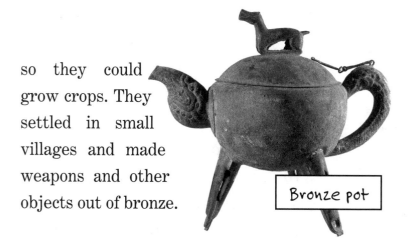

Bronze pot

Dynasties

In the beginning, China was not one country. Rulers from powerful families controlled different parts of the land. They had their own armies and created *dynasties* (DY-nuh-steez) that often lasted hundreds of years. The last dynasty ended only about a hundred years ago.

A dynasty is a series of rulers from the same family that stays in power for a long time.

The rulers lived in palaces with servants, gardens, and beautiful objects. Since the Chinese believed that their spirits lived on after they died, the rulers' tombs were filled with works of

21

art, cooking pots, clothes, jewelry, weapons, and even food.

Chinese Thought

In 1046 BC, the powerful Zhou (JOH) dynasty took over a large part of the country. It was the longest dynasty in Chinese history and lasted until 256 BC.

During this time in China, wise men called philosophers (fih-LOSS-uh-furz) began to seriously think and write about how people should live.

Two of the greatest Chinese philosophers were Laozi (LOW-dzuh) and Confucius (cunn-FYOO-shuss). Their ideas are still important today, not only in China but all over the world.

Laozi lived around 600 BC. He began the philosophy of Daoism (DOW-iz-um).

22

Laozi

One of its teachings is that people and everything in nature share the same life force. Because of this, Laozi believed we should live in peace and harmony. Laozi also taught that everyone needed a balance between action and stillness.

Confucius is the most famous philosopher China has ever had. He was born in

A scholar is someone who learns a lot by studying hard.

551 BC. Confucius was a teacher and a *scholar* (SKAHL-ur). He believed in honoring old Chinese ways. These included respect for elders and the need for strong families and education.

Confucius

Confucius said that if people followed rules of good behavior, there would be order. He didn't think that governments should make a lot of strict laws. Confucius also taught people to respect one another, honor their ancestors, and live peacefully.

Many other philosophers lived during the Zhou dynasty. Like Laozi and Confucius, they wrote books and began schools of philosophy. In Chinese history, this time is known as the golden age of Chinese philosophy.

Every year thousands of people visit Qufu, the birthplace of Confucius.

Timeline of Dynasties

Periods of Chinese history are known as dynasties.

- **2070–1600 BC: Xia**
  First dynasty in China
- **1600–1046 BC: Shang**
  First dynasty to leave written records
- **1046–256 BC: Zhou**
  Golden age of philosophy
- **221–207 BC: Qin**
  First emperor of all of China, Great Wall
- **206 BC–AD 220: Han**
  Invention of paper
- **AD 300–589: Six Dynasties**

Different dynasties
ruling at the same time
— AD 589–617: Sui
— AD 618–907: Tang
   Invention of woodblock
   printing
— AD 907–960: Five Dynasties
— AD 960–1279: Song
   Invention of moveable
   type and compass
— AD 1279–1368: Yuan
— AD 1368–1644: Ming
   Beijing becomes capital
— AD 1644–1912: Qing
   Last dynasty

2

Rise of the First Emperor

When the Zhou dynasty ended, seven states began competing to control China. This is known as the era of the Warring States.

In 230 BC, Ying Zheng, the king of the state of Qin (CHIN), declared war on the other six states. His armies attacked each of them one by one. By 221 BC, he had defeated all of them.

Ying Zheng was now the first person to rule all of China. His empire spread out over one million square miles! To mark this huge event, he changed his title to Qin Shihuangdi, which means "First Emperor of China." But it can also mean something bigger—like ruler of the whole universe!

Building a Country

Each of the states had been running things its own way. They all had their own kinds of money. Their laws and customs were often different, and people spoke different forms of Chinese. To unite the country, Qin Shihuangdi had to make things the same across China.

The Government

The emperor began by setting up thirty-six districts, or areas, all over the country to govern the people. He sent his best officials to run them. Under his direction, these men controlled the farms and the army. They also made sure people obeyed the emperor of Qin's laws and paid taxes.

The Same Way

Qin Shihuangdi ordered everyone to measure and weigh things with the same system. People were to buy things with the same kind of money and write in the same form of Chinese.

In order to connect all of China to the capital, the emperor had many miles of roads built. Axles on wagons, chariots, and carriages had to be the same size so that vehicles could move easily. To make traveling by boat faster, he also built canals that joined rivers together.

A <u>capital</u> city is where the main government is. Qin's was Xianyang (SHEN-yung) in central China.

31

Qin Shihuangdi, the All Powerful

To keep all the power, the emperor of Qin took land away from ruling families across the country. Then he moved about 120,000 members of those families to palaces in Xianyang so he could keep an eye on them!

The Summer Palace in Beijing is a great example of an old Chinese palace.

The emperor's rule was enforced by a loyal army of over 600,000 soldiers who stood by to carry out his orders.

Legalism

The emperor of Qin was a legalist. Legalism was one of the philosophies that began during the Zhou dynasty. Legalists believed that people were basically bad and the government needed to make strict laws for them.

Qin Shihuangdi's rules were harsh. People didn't have fair trials. They were often tortured to confess to even the smallest crimes, and sent away to work on building projects.

The emperor's secret police force watched out for lawbreakers. And ordinary people were supposed to spy on their neighbors and fellow workers.

Qin Shihuangdi's actions made his subjects so angry that some even planned to kill him. One time, he thought his mother was plotting against him. He sent her to live far away from the capital. He also sent away one of his sons!

Qin Shihuangdi had many sons and wives.

Burn the Books!

The emperor ordered scholars to burn every book that didn't agree with his ideas. These included books of history, philosophy, poetry, and literature.

Among the books tossed into the bonfires were those of Confucius.

Books on practical things, like farming and medicine, weren't burned.

Yikes! If Confucius's books were burned, how do we know about his teachings?

A few private copies survived. Some books were memorized and copied down later.

The emperor punished scholars who did not burn the books. He ordered over four hundred to be buried alive! Others had their faces tattooed to show that they were guilty. They were sent away to work on the emperor's building projects.

Scholars had always been respected in ancient China. These terrible acts made people hate Qin Shihuangdi even more.

Burying the scholars

The Great Wall of China

For years, fierce tribes had attacked China's northern border. Over the years, rulers built walls to keep them out.

Qin Shihuangdi wanted one massive wall all the way across the northern Chinese border. It would have to go over mountains and through deserts, swamps, and forests.

The emperor ordered thousands of prisoners, peasants, and soldiers to start building it. The men worked in terrible heat and bitter cold. Thousands died from illness, exhaustion, or injuries.

It took about twelve years to finish 1,500 miles of wall. It didn't cover the entire border, and the cost was huge. So many workers died that the wall was known as "the cemetery wall."

Time and the weather destroyed

There are some estimates that over 400,000 people died building the wall.

37

the emperor's wall. Almost no traces of it remain today. It wasn't until the 1570s that a Great Wall that stretched across the border of northern China was completed.

Today, the Great Wall covers over 5,500 miles. It is one of the biggest building projects in human history. Millions come from all over the world to look at it in awe and wonder.

President Barack Obama visited the Great Wall in November 2009.

The Dragon Kings

Since 3000 BC, dragons have been symbols of good fortune and strength in China. Even today, pictures and statues of dragons are everywhere. Although they look fierce, the Chinese think of them as kind and friendly.

In ancient China, people believed that dragons kept evil spirits away and granted people long lives. Chinese dragons took different forms. Some had wings, while others lived in the water. Some were believed to guard rivers, create wind, and produce rain and crops.

Chinese rulers often called themselves dragon kings. Their faces were known as dragon faces, their thrones as dragon thrones, and they wore dragon robes. The emperor of Qin surely thought he was the greatest dragon of all! (But he wasn't the friendliest.)

3

The Terra-Cotta Soldiers

In 210 BC, Qin Shihuangdi was far away from the capital, inspecting his empire. Suddenly he got sick and died. His officials worried that news of his death might start a revolt. They decided to keep it a secret.

They put the emperor in his chariot and pretended he was alive. To fool people, they brought food and messages to him. But the weather was hot, and the body began to smell.

His men had a bright idea. They loaded

rotten fish in a cart and sent it just ahead of the chariot. Along the way, people thought it was the fish that they smelled, not their emperor.

Workers had been building Qin Shihuangdi's tomb since he was a boy. It was in central China, near the capital at the foot of Mount Lishan. The emperor was buried in it when he was only forty-nine years old.

One of Qin Shihuangdi's sons became the next emperor. Because people hated Qin Shihuangdi, they rose up against his son. The Qin dynasty had lasted just fifteen years.

After many years, the emperor's tomb was almost forgotten. By the twentieth century, no one knew where the exact location was.

A Great Discovery

March 1974 was a dry month in central China. Some farmers were digging a well to water their crops. Suddenly one of them struck something hard with his hoe. To his surprise, he uncovered a life-size clay statue of a man's head!

The farmers also found bronze objects and pottery.

Yang Zhifa was one of the farmers who found the tomb.

Archaeologists (ahr-kee-ALL-uh-jists) examined the head and other items the farmers brought to them. They said that the objects were over 2,000 years old. They dated back to the reign of the emperor of Qin!

A team of archaeologists went out to check the spot where the farmers had dug up the head. They realized that this was where Qin Shihuangdi was buried. They discovered that his burial site was the size of a small city! The project that they started more than forty years ago is so huge that it's still going on today.

The Terra-Cotta Soldiers

The farmers had found the head of a soldier statue made of terra-cotta. Archaeologists have uncovered about 8,000

terra-cotta soldiers so far! The emperor created an army of them to guard his tomb. They are in three pits about a mile away from it.

The first pit is more than twice the size of a football field. It holds about 6,000 soldiers. The second pit has about 1,500 soldiers and horses. The third is the smallest, with only sixty-eight men and a single team of horses. This was probably meant to be the command post. Statues dressed as generals look as if they are planning an attack.

The Soldiers

The soldiers stand in straight lines with dirt walls on either side. No two are alike. They are all different ages and sizes. Their heights range from 5 feet 11 inches to over 6 feet tall. Some have beards. Some are smiling, and others are frowning. Even their hair and beards aren't alike. The statues were supposed to look like real men in the emperor's army.

Patches of paint on them show that they were once painted in bright colors. The paint is so fragile, it falls apart only a short time after contact with the air.

High-ranking officers are taller to show their importance.

Ready to Fight

The soldiers wear their uniforms and are lined up in a perfect battle formation. The generals wear ornate uniforms while

General

49

 The terra-cotta horses look like the strong little Mongolian ponies that the Chinese used.

bowmen are dressed in simple jackets that come to their knees.

War chariots, terra-cotta horses, and real bronze and iron weapons are buried with the statues. The weapons include crossbows, spears, and swords. Some of the weapons are still sharp!

Archaeologists have found over 40,000 bronze arrowheads.

The Soldiers Today

In the late 1970s, the Chinese put buildings over the pits to protect the statues. Every year, thousands come to see the emperor of Qin's amazing army. They also watch craftsmen at work repairing broken statues and making models of them.

The Emperor's Tomb

Old reports say that the workers set up booby traps of loaded crossbows. They were aimed at the entrance, ready to fire if anyone entered the tomb.

Mercury is a poisonous silvery metal that is liquid at room temperature.

Today, Qin Shihuangdi's tomb remains sealed. After he was buried, workers covered it with tons of dirt. His body lies in the middle of the tomb. The ancient Chinese thought that jade preserved bodies, so his is probably covered in a suit of jade.

During the Han dynasty, a famous Chinese historian named Sima Qian wrote that the tomb was like a palace. The floor's design looked like China's rivers and mountains. The ceiling had paintings of the sun, moon, and stars.

Sima Qian reported that a machine caused rivers of mercury to flow around the tomb, which were supposed to stand for the great rivers of China.

Scientists have tested the soil near the tomb and found a high mercury reading, so this may be true!

This wax figure of Sima Qian is on dispaly at the National Museum of China.

Archaeologists won't open the tomb until they can do so safely, without destroying what's inside. After all these years, the tomb of the first emperor of China remains a mystery. Who knows what incredible treasures might lie inside?

Qin Shihuangdi and the Elixir of Life

The emperor of Qin was really afraid of dying. He had reason to be. People had tried to kill him at least three times! All his life, the emperor searched for a potion to help him live forever. The potion he wanted is known as the elixir of life.

He tried eating all kinds of things in hopes of living forever. Some of them, such as a mixture of powdered jade and mercury, may actually have killed him.

The emperor heard that people on an island near China had magical herbs that helped them stay young forever. He ordered a famous wizard name Xu Fu to find this island and bring the elixir back with him.

Xu Fu chose several thousand boys and girls to go with him. They climbed aboard sixty small boats and pushed out to sea. Not one of them ever returned. Legend says that Xu Fu discovered Japan. There are stories that he actually became its very first emperor.

4

Great Inventions

The Chinese invented many things long before any other country. Over 4,000 years ago, for example, they discovered the art of making silk.

The story goes that Leizu, wife of the Emperor Huangdi, was sipping tea under a mulberry tree. Suddenly a mulberry caterpillar's cocoon dropped into her cup. The cocoon came apart in the warm water. Its threads were beautiful and shiny.

The empress began to think that cloth could be made from this caterpillar's cocoon. She was right. Women workers began growing mulberry caterpillars on special farms. After the caterpillars spun their cocoons, the women boiled the cocoons to get silk threads.

At first, only royal families could wear silk. It was so prized that it sometimes took the place of money.

Wow! One cocoon could make 1,200 yards of silk thread!

Since mulberry silk moths lived in China and no other country, the Chinese kept the secret of how to make silk from the rest of the world. Anyone caught smuggling silk worms out of the country was risking his life!

For over 2,000 years, China alone produced silk. Finally the secret was out, and Japan and Korea got into the silk-making business as well.

The Chinese also came up with lots of other things we still use today. Wheelbarrows, umbrellas, and noodles were all invented in China!

Let's go see what else the Chinese invented!

Paper

Long ago, there was no paper, and people used bones, bark, shells, strips of bamboo, and reeds instead.

In AD 105, a Chinese official named Cai Lun found a way to make the first real paper. First he soaked bits of mulberry bark, old fishing nets, and hemp cloth in water. Then he squeezed out all the water and dried it in thin sheets in the sun. Cai Lun had invented paper!

Because they had paper, the Chinese were the first to use toilet paper, tea bags, paper napkins, and paper money. And when people wanted to give gifts, they tucked money into a paper envelope!

Printing

In early China, people wrote everything out by hand. This took so much time that usually there was only one copy of a book or document. If people needed more, they hired a scribe.

Around AD 600, the Chinese started carving words on wooden blocks. They put ink on the blocks and pushed paper down onto them. When they lifted the paper, it had writing on it. This process is called block printing. It helped, but it was still slow going.

In 1048, Pi Sheng carved separate words on pieces of clay. Then he glued the words on iron boards and printed from them with ink. Afterward, he could break the letters off and use them again.

Later, wood and then bronze were used for the letters instead of clay. Copying things was cheaper, easier, and faster. It wasn't until about 400 years later that Johannes Gutenberg invented moveable type in Europe.

Compass

Early people looked at the sun and the stars to tell where they were going. Today we use a compass as our guide. It tells us which direction is north, south, east, and west.

By the eleventh century, the Chinese invented the first compass. It was used by sailors and was a magnetic needle floating on water. The needle pointed north and gave sailors an idea of where they were headed. They still used the stars and sun, but on cloudy days, a compass really helped.

Later, the Chinese came up with a "dry compass" that didn't need water. Once people learned to use it, they drew better maps. Once they had maps, they could go almost anywhere they wanted to go!

Gunpowder

In AD 850, the Chinese were still trying to make an elixir of life. They found that one of their powders caused fires and explosions. They even burned down a building with it!

Instead of an elixir, the scientists had discovered gunpowder. Gunpowder changed warfare forever. At first, soldiers tied gunpowder packets to arrows and sent them flying toward the enemy. Later, gunpowder became firepower for cannons, guns, and rockets.

In the seventh century, the Chinese discovered that mixing gunpowder with color makes fireworks. What began as a search for life wound up creating weapons for war, but it also gave us great shows in the night skies!

Ship Rudders

The early Chinese steered boats with oars. Since it was such hard work, their boats were small. In the first century AD, the Chinese invented rudders.

A rudder is a flat piece of wood or metal attached to the back of a boat. Part of the rudder stays in the water. A shaft or pole connects it to a wheel on the deck. Sailors on the ship can steer it in different directions by turning the wheel.

Rudders allowed the Chinese to build larger ships. This helped them trade and sell more goods to countries like Japan and Korea. They also built powerful naval warships that ruled the seas around China for years.

Porcelain

Museums often have beautiful Chinese vases and bowls made thousands of years ago. This type of pottery is called *porcelain* (PORE-suh-lin).

Around AD 700, the Chinese heated a special clay called kaolin up to very high temperatures. The pottery they created was strong but so fine that light could shine through it. At first, potters made useful things like bowls and cups. Later, during the Tang dynasty, making porcelain objects became an art.

Chinese craftsmen made incredible glazed and painted statues, bowls, and vases that were sold in Asia and later throughout Europe. (For years, porcelain plates have been called fine china.)

In 2010, an eighteenth-century Chinese porcelain vase sold for over $69 million! It had been in a family's dusty attic for years, but no one realized how valuable it was. What a great surprise!

5

Daily Life in China

Daily life in China today is very busy. People work hard and have little free time. In spite of this, they take time for good manners. They have practiced them for hundreds, if not thousands, of years.

Parents begin teaching their children how to behave when they are very young. In school, they must take classes in manners.

Students learn how to eat properly, how

to line up the right way, and how to treat their elders with respect. Their teachers also show them the polite way to write letters and emails.

It's part of the Chinese culture to honor teachers. When a teacher walks into the

On September 10, schoolchildren celebrate Teachers' Day by bringing little presents to their teachers.

class, students stand up, bow, and say "*Laoshihao*," which means "Hello, teacher." They would never think of talking back to their teachers. That's considered very bad manners!

Meeting and Greeting

Although handshaking is becoming more popular, when many Chinese meet one another, they bow and sometimes look down at the ground to show respect. They also greet the eldest person first.

Children bow or nod their heads as a sign of respect to grown-ups. If someone is just a little older than they are, they might call that person "big brother" or "big sister" instead of their real names. They often address old people as "grandmother" or "grandfather" even if they aren't related.

Food

After the Chinese say hello to their friends, to be really polite, they'll ask if the other person has eaten that day. Food has always been a big part of Chinese culture.

The kind of food people eat in China depends on where they live. There are eight main types of cooking.

Everyone eats with chopsticks, even little children.

In Sichuan (sitch-WAHN) Province, for example, people enjoy spicy food with salty, sweet, and sour flavors. Food in the Canton region of southern China is supposed to be some of the best in the world. Friends often meet in restaurants or houses to enjoy tasty dishes of fish, tofu, vegetables, noodles, and rice.

They also eat some things that you wouldn't believe, like stir-fried hairy gourd,

When we visit China, we'll show good manners by doing these things:

1. We'll take off our shoes when we visit someone's home.
2. We'll bring a little present and hold it in both hands when we give it to our host.

frog legs wrapped in lotus leaves, chicken feet, and jellyfish!

3. We'll hold our chopsticks correctly.

4. When we eat rice, we'll hold the bowl up to our mouth and shovel in the rice with chopsticks.

5. We'll show that we enjoy our food by burping and slurping!

6. We'll take some of everything that is offered to us, even if we don't like it. And then we'll smile and say <u>"xie, xie"</u> (SHE-ah SHE-ah), which means "thank you."

Kids and Schools

Chinese students work hard in school, especially in cities. If they want good jobs later, they need good educations and must be at the top of their class to go to college.

Students start their day early, waking up sometimes at 5:30 or 6:00 in the

Kids usually wear uniforms in school.

morning. After a breakfast of congee or rice, they head out the door. Their days are long. Monday through Friday classes last for about nine hours. Many kids take extra lessons in math or English after school and on Saturday.

Congee is a porridge made from rice.

They learn math, science, history, literature, and English. At night, they often have so much homework that they have to stay up late to get it all done.

All of this work is paying off. Chinese kids beat many other countries on tests. Now if they could only get a little sleep. . . . *Zzzzz.*

Many older students have twelve-hour days!

Families

China is so crowded that the government wants parents to have only one child.

Confucius's idea of the father as head of the house is still true in most families. Modern fathers guide their children with a firm hand but are not as strict as they were in the past.

Grandparents, parents, and children often live together in one house. Since

both parents usually work, grandparents often take care of the children and do the cleaning and cooking.

Young Chinese adults usually live with their parents until they get married. In spite of all the changes in their country, Chinese people still value family ties more than anything else.

It is a custom in China for elderly parents to live with their children.

Chinese Language

The Chinese speak about 220 different dialects, or types of Chinese. The official language is Mandarin. Children use Mandarin in school, and more people speak it than any other language in the world, including English.

The Chinese don't have an alphabet. Instead, people write characters or symbols for words. There are over 20,000 of them! People should know at least 2,000 characters just to read on a basic level. Most people usually learn about 5,000.

Some Chinese words look the same but mean different things. People know the meaning by the tone of voice someone uses when they say them.

6

Celebrate!

Throughout their history, the Chinese have celebrated important dates with festivals. Their biggest festival is Chinese New Year.

For the Chinese, New Year begins on the second new moon after the longest day of the year. That's because the Chinese calendar is different from ours. It's a lunar calendar, which means it's based on the phases of the moon. Many celebrations happen on important dates in the lunar calendar.

Each year in the Chinese calendar is named for one of twelve animals in the Chinese *zodiac*. Every twelve years, the cycle of animals begins again.

The Chinese believe people share

The zodiac is believed to be a way to guide people about their future actions. What animal sign are you?

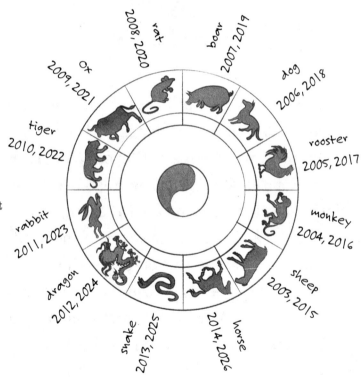

rat 2008, 2020

boar 2007, 2019

ox 2009, 2021

dog 2006, 2018

tiger 2010, 2022

rooster 2005, 2017

monkey 2004, 2016

rabbit 2011, 2023

sheep 2003, 2015

dragon 2012, 2024

snake 2013, 2025

horse 2014, 2026

88

some of the same behaviors as their animal sign. For example, 2014 is the Year of the Horse. People born during this time are thought to be friendly, popular, and fond of traveling. When the Chinese wish people good health, they might greet them by saying "the spirit of the dragon and horse!"

Chinese New Year

Everyone starts preparing for the New Year's festival weeks ahead of time. They send cards and poems to their friends with good wishes for the coming year. Sometimes they tape copies of their favorite poems on their front door.

Since the Chinese consider their new year to be the first month of spring, it's also called Spring Festival.

Many stores close at noon on New Year's Eve so people can get ready for the evening. That night, friends and

families gather to eat delicious food. The skies light up with fireworks and lots of firecrackers are set off.

The next day, parents give their children red envelopes filled with money called lucky money. People wear red clothes and hang red decorations in their houses. They spend the day offering gifts to their ancestors, visiting temples, or watching dancers dressed as dragons doing dragon dances and beating drums to frighten off evil spirits.

Festival of Pure Brightness

In April each year, families head out to graveyards to clean up their ancestors' graves. This is known as the Festival of Pure Brightness, or Tomb Sweeping Day. For well over a thousand years, the Chinese have honored their ancestors this way.

People bring offerings of food to the graves. They light incense, pray, and burn candles at the gravesites. Then the family sits down next to the graves and enjoys a big picnic. Kids fly kites, and everyone relaxes in the warm spring air.

Dragon Boat Festival

For over 2,000 years, the Chinese have held a Dragon Boat Festival. Boats carved like brightly colored dragons race against one another. As the crowds cheer, drumbeats sound out every stroke of the oars.

This festival is also a celebration of good health. Many people wear sweet-smelling bags of herbs around their

During the races, people eat rice dumplings called zongzi, which are shaped like pyramids.

necks, take long walks, and hang bunches of herbs on doors.

There's a belief that if someone can balance an egg on one end exactly at noon on Boat Festival day, the coming year will be a happy one.

Kite Festival

The Chinese invented kites over 2,800 years ago. The first were made of silk, and soldiers used them to signal each other. Later, the Chinese began making paper kites. Today the skies in China are often alive with colorful kites flying in the breeze.

The city of Weifang is known as the kite capital of the world. Every spring, it holds a six-day kite festival. The most amazing kites in all different shapes and sizes soar through the air at the festival. There are usually tiger, butterfly, and octopus kites. And of course there are lots and lots of dragons!

Moon Festival

After harvesting their crops in the fall, the Chinese celebrate the harvest during the autumn full moon. The moon is a symbol of peace and togetherness. Families and friends gather to gaze at the full moon as it rises in the night sky.

Everyone enjoys eating special cakes called moon cakes during the festival.

Children try to catch a glimpse of Chang'e, the Moon Goddess. She is said to be a beautiful dancer living on the moon with a jade rabbit as her only companion.

In 2007, a Chinese spacecraft sent to explore the moon was named Chang'e.

Birthday Celebrations

Soon after the birth of a baby, the parents stand before the family shrine to tell

When a Chinese baby is born, he or she is already said to be a year old.

their ancestors that there's a new member of the family.

A month after babies are born, they have their very first birthday party. The parents give friends and relatives dyed red eggs as a symbol for a happy life. Their friends bring gifts like food, silver, gold, or money wrapped up in bright red paper. That night, the parents host a delicious dinner for everyone at a restaurant.

But it's usually a long time before people have another birthday party again. They have to wait until they are sixty! Then there's a big family party. People eat eggs and long-life noodles. They bring presents and toast the birthday man or woman. The older you are, the bigger your birthday is in China.

After turning sixty, people have to

wait for another ten years, and then it's time to celebrate their birthday again. Imagine what a great party you'd have if you lived to be one hundred!

Zhuazhou

A year after babies are born, parents hold a ceremony called Zhuazhou. It's supposed to tell them what their child will be in the future.

Parents put lots of objects on a table or tray in front of the baby. They might include spoons, books, paper, pens, coins, flowers, food, and toys.

Everyone watches as the baby reaches for something. If the child grabs a toy, for example, people think he or she will enjoy having fun. If a book is chosen, they believe the baby will be a good student.

Zhuazhou has been a custom in China for thousands of years. Today, most parents do it to celebrate their children and to keep an old tradition alive.

7

Chinese Around the World

Chinese people live all over the world. Today, cities in Thailand, Canada, Indonesia, Australia, and the United States have many Chinese residents. Wherever the Chinese are, they take their customs with them.

In cities like New York City, Los Angeles, Chicago, and San Francisco, many Chinese live together in areas called Chinatowns. Walking down the streets of any Chinatown makes you think you are actually in China. There are Chinese restaurants where friends enjoy eating dishes such as Peking duck and fried rice.

In the early morning, the parks are full of folks doing Chinese exercises like Tai Chi or playing a game with small tiles called mah-jongg. On Chinese New Year, celebrations go on just as they do in China.

Almost every Chinatown is full of the smells, sights, and sounds of China. If you can't get to China, China can come to you!

Gifts from China

Besides its great inventions, China has given great art to the world. Today, we can see incredible Chinese landscape paintings and porcelain in many museums.

We might take courses in Chinese calligraphy and learn to master some Chinese characters with ink and a brush. In almost every bookstore or library, there are books on Chinese poetry and art. The culture of China has made our own culture richer in many ways.

The Chinese began writing beautiful poems over 2,000 years ago.

China's Future

China has changed faster than almost any other country. Within a very short time, it's grown into a major power. Its official name now is the People's Republic of China. The Chinese have proven that they have some of the best workers in the world, and they are building a great future.

China might send rockets into space, but its people also treasure many things from the past. They still eat noodles and rice with chopsticks. They still read great philosophers like Confucius, and they still honor their ancestors.

Doing More Research

There's a lot more you can learn about ancient China. The fun of research is seeing how many different sources you can explore.

Books

Most libraries and bookstores have books about China.

Here are some things to remember when you're using books for research:

1. You don't have to read the whole book. Check the table of contents and the index to find the topics you're interested in.

2. Write down the name of the book.

When you take notes, make sure you write down the name of the book in your notebook so you can find it again.

3. Never copy exactly from a book.

When you learn something new from a book, put it in your own words.

4. Make sure the book is <u>nonfiction</u>.

Some books tell make-believe stories about ancient China. Make-believe stories are called *fiction*. They're fun to read, but not good for research.

Research books have facts and tell true stories. They are called *nonfiction*. A librarian or teacher can help you make sure the books you use for research are nonfiction.

Here are some good nonfiction books about China:

- *DK Eyewitness: Ancient China* by Arthur Cotterell

- *DK Eyewitness: China* by Hugh Sebag-Montefiore

- *The Great Wall* by Elizabeth Mann

- *Growing Up in Ancient China* by Ken Teague

- *Hidden Army: Clay Soldiers of Ancient China* by Jane O'Connor

- *The Story of Silk: From Worm Spit to Woven Scarves* by Richard Sobol

- *You Wouldn't Want to Work on the Great Wall of China! Defenses You'd Rather Not Build* by Jacqueline Morley

Museums and Chinatowns

Many museums and Chinatowns can help you learn more about Chinese culture.

When you go to a museum:

1. Be sure to take your notebook!
Write down anything that catches your interest. Draw pictures, too!

2. Ask questions.
There are almost always people at museums who can help you find what you're looking for.

3. Check the calendar.
Many museums have special events and activities just for kids!

Here are some museums that have exhibits about China:

- Asian Art Museum of San Francisco

- Children's Museum of Indianapolis

- Chinese-American Museum of Chicago

- Cleveland Museum of Art

- Metropolitan Museum of Art
  (New York City)

- Museum of Chinese in America
  (New York City)

- Museum of Fine Arts, Boston

There are many things to do and see in a Chinatown. You can try Chinese food at a restaurant, or watch a game of mah-jongg in the park. Before you visit, check if any festivals or street parades are happening while you are there.

These cities have Chinatowns you might like to visit:

• Boston

• Chicago

• Los Angeles

• New York City

• San Francisco

• Seattle

DVDs

There are some great nonfiction DVDs about ancient China. As with books, make sure the DVDs you watch for research are nonfiction!

Check your library or video store for these and other nonfiction titles about China:

- *China's First Emperor* from the History Channel

- *Modern Marvels: The Great Wall of China* from the History Channel

- *Secrets of China's First Emperor* from E1 Entertainment

- *Secrets of the Dead: China Terracotta Warriors* from PBS

The Internet

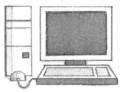

Many websites have lots of facts about ancient China. Some also have games and activities that can help make learning about China even more fun.

Ask your teacher or your parents to help you find more websites like these:

- china.mrdonn.org
- ducksters.com/history/china /ancient_china.php
- enchantedlearning.com/asia/china
- great-wallofchina.com/china-facts -for-kids.html
- historyforkids.net/ancient-china.html

Good luck!

Index

Photographs courtesy of:

Don't miss Magic Tree House®
Super Edition #1
Danger in the Darkest Hour

Jack and Annie travel to Normandy,
France during World War II for their
most dangerous mission ever!

Have you read the adventure that matches up with this book?

Don't miss Magic Tree House® #14
Day of the Dragon King

Jack and Annie travel back to ancient China. There, a powerful emperor called the Dragon King has ordered that all books be burned. Will Jack and Annie be able to save at least one book? Or will they be captured by the emperor's soldiers?

Want even more
Magic Tree House® fun?

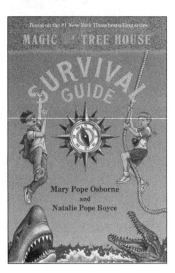

Magic Tree House® Books

#1: DINOSAURS BEFORE DARK
#2: THE KNIGHT AT DAWN
#3: MUMMIES IN THE MORNING
#4: PIRATES PAST NOON
#5: NIGHT OF THE NINJAS
#6: AFTERNOON ON THE AMAZON
#7: SUNSET OF THE SABERTOOTH
#8: MIDNIGHT ON THE MOON
#9: DOLPHINS AT DAYBREAK
#10: GHOST TOWN AT SUNDOWN
#11: LIONS AT LUNCHTIME
#12: POLAR BEARS PAST BEDTIME
#13: VACATION UNDER THE VOLCANO
#14: DAY OF THE DRAGON KING
#15: VIKING SHIPS AT SUNRISE
#16: HOUR OF THE OLYMPICS
#17: TONIGHT ON THE *TITANIC*
#18: BUFFALO BEFORE BREAKFAST
#19: TIGERS AT TWILIGHT
#20: DINGOES AT DINNERTIME
#21: CIVIL WAR ON SUNDAY
#22: REVOLUTIONARY WAR ON WEDNESDAY
#23: TWISTER ON TUESDAY
#24: EARTHQUAKE IN THE EARLY MORNING
#25: STAGE FRIGHT ON A SUMMER NIGHT
#26: GOOD MORNING, GORILLAS
#27: THANKSGIVING ON THURSDAY
#28: HIGH TIDE IN HAWAII

Merlin Missions

#29: CHRISTMAS IN CAMELOT
#30: HAUNTED CASTLE ON HALLOWS EVE
#31: SUMMER OF THE SEA SERPENT
#32: WINTER OF THE ICE WIZARD
#33: CARNIVAL AT CANDLELIGHT
#34: SEASON OF THE SANDSTORMS
#35: NIGHT OF THE NEW MAGICIANS
#36: BLIZZARD OF THE BLUE MOON
#37: DRAGON OF THE RED DAWN
#38: MONDAY WITH A MAD GENIUS
#39: DARK DAY IN THE DEEP SEA
#40: EVE OF THE EMPEROR PENGUIN
#41: MOONLIGHT ON THE MAGIC FLUTE

#42: A GOOD NIGHT FOR GHOSTS
#43: LEPRECHAUN IN LATE WINTER
#44: A GHOST TALE FOR CHRISTMAS TIME
#45: A CRAZY DAY WITH COBRAS
#46: DOGS IN THE DEAD OF NIGHT
#47: ABE LINCOLN AT LAST!
#48: A PERFECT TIME FOR PANDAS
#49: STALLION BY STARLIGHT
#50: HURRY UP, HOUDINI!
#51: HIGH TIME FOR HEROES
#52: SOCCER ON SUNDAY

Magic Tree House® Fact Trackers

Dinosaurs
Knights and Castles
Mummies and Pyramids
Pirates
Rain Forests
Space
Titanic
Twisters and Other Terrible Storms
Dolphins and Sharks
Ancient Greece and the Olympics
American Revolution
Sabertooths and the Ice Age
Pilgrims
Ancient Rome and Pompeii
Tsunamis and Other Natural Disasters
Polar Bears and the Arctic
Sea Monsters
Penguins and Antarctica
Leonardo da Vinci
Ghosts
Leprechauns and Irish Folklore
Rags and Riches: Kids in the Time of Charles Dickens
Snakes and Other Reptiles
Dog Heroes
Abraham Lincoln
Pandas and Other Endangered Species
Horse Heroes
Heroes for All Times
Soccer
Ninjas and Samurai
China: Land of the Emperor's Great Wall

More Magic Tree House®

Games and Puzzles from the Tree House
Magic Tricks from the Tree House
My Magic Tree House Journal
Magic Tree House Survival Guide

BRING MAGIC TREE HOUSE TO YOUR SCHOOL!

Magic Tree House musicals now available for performance by young people!

Ask your teacher or director to contact Music Theatre International for more information:
BroadwayJr.com
Licensing@MTIshows.com
(212) 541-4684

MAGIC TREE HOUSE COLLECTION
DINOSAURS BEFORE DARK KIDS

MAGIC TREE HOUSE COLLECTION
The Knight at Dawn KIDS

ATTENTION, TEACHERS!

Mary Pope Osborne's
Classroom Adventures Program

The Magic Tree House **CLASSROOM ADVENTURES PROGRAM** is a free, comprehensive set of online educational resources for teachers developed by Mary Pope Osborne as a gift to teachers, to thank them for their enthusiastic support of the series. Educators can learn more at MTHClassroomAdventures.org.